IMAGES
of Sports

THE NEW YORK
RANGERS

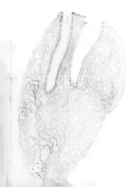

JUBILATION ALL AROUND. Madison Square Garden was officially rocking as captain Mark Messier and his band of happy teammates circled the ice with the fourth Stanley Cup in Rangers history on June 14, 1994. A moment later, Messier passed the cup itself into the crowd. Fifty-four years of waiting was over. The cup was theirs, and tears flowed. (Photograph courtesy of George Kalinsky.)

IMAGES
of Sports

THE NEW YORK
RANGERS

John Halligan

ARCADIA
PUBLISHING

Copyright © 2003 by John Halligan
ISBN 978-0-7385-1228-0

Published by Arcadia Publishing
Charleston, South Carolina

Printed in the United States of America

Library of Congress Catalog Card Number: 2003104863

For all general information contact Arcadia Publishing at:
Telephone 843-853-2070
Fax 843-853-0044
E-mail sales@arcadiapublishing.com
For customer service and orders:
Toll-Free 1-888-313-2665

Visit us on the Internet at www.arcadiapublishing.com

HE GOT THE PICTURE. Resourceful photographer Barton Silverman of the *New York Times*, shown here in training camp in 1967, always got the picture he wanted, even if it meant putting himself in peril. Much of Silverman's work is featured in this volume. (Photograph by Bob Glass.)

CONTENTS

ACKNOWLEDGMENTS

All of the images herein, with precious few exceptions as noted, are from the archives of the New York Rangers and reprinted with the team's permission. The photographs are more than just a history of a hockey team. They are, in fact, a tribute and a paean to the remarkable photojournalists who have chronicled the Rangers for nearly 80 years.

Chief among the photographic "artistes" who have contributed their work to the Rangers archive, mostly on assignment but sometimes as freelancers, are Barton Silverman, Bruce Bennett, Melchior diGiacomo, and George Kalinsky, the best of the best. But there were others as well, friends all: Bob Glass, Jerry Liebman, Rich Pilling, Peter and Jack Mecca (pictured below), Paul Bereswill, Joe Bereswill, Dan Baliotti, Victor Mikus, Louis Requena, Chuck Solomon, Ray Amati, John Tremmel, and Nury Hernandez. This book celebrates their work and is dedicated to them all, and also to my wife, Janet.

In addition, I would like to thank the late Herb Goren and the late Stan Saplin, who taught me (plus countless others) the need to preserve the photographic, written, and electronic history of a great game and a great team. Thanks also to Don O'Hanley, whose sage advice and perspective adds greatly to any hockey project. Plus, without the support of the Rangers organization, this project would not have even been started.

(Photograph by Melchior diGiacomo.)

INTRODUCTION

The New York Rangers have always been a team of the people of New York City, of course, but also of the suburbs and the region. Nothing demonstrated that more dramatically than team captain Mark Messier passing the Stanley Cup itself into the crowd for the fans to touch and savor while Madison Square Garden continued to roar nearly 20 minutes after the 1994 championship.

The team's love affair with New York and environs has not lessened, not even with the arrival of the New York Islanders in 1972 and the New Jersey Devils in 1982. These events, in fact, merely steeled two of the finest rivalries in all of hockey between the Rangers and each of the neighboring teams.

At their inception in 1926, the Rangers were an instant hit with the people of New York. They attracted a formally dressed crowd (dinner jackets for the men, gowns for the women). The games began at 8:45 p.m., coinciding with curtain time for the nearby Broadway theaters.

Success for the Rangers came quickly. They earned a Stanley Cup in only their second season, 1927–1928, another in 1932–1933, and a third in 1939–1940. Support for the Rangers grew and developed into one of the most rabid fan bases in all of sports, including a formal fan club that has been cheering the team for more than half a century.

The Rangers play in Madison Square Garden, "the world's most famous arena." This volume celebrates, in pictures and in words, both the Rangers and the Garden.

WHAT THEY PLAY FOR. The Stanley Cup is the most famous trophy in professional sports. More than 1,000 National Hockey League players compete for it on an annual basis. The Rangers have won the Stanley Cup four times in 77 seasons: 1928, 1933, 1940, and 1994.

One

THE BIRTH OF A FRANCHISE

TRADITION ON ICE. It is a logo that is recognized around the world. It has remained essentially unchanged for 78 years, except for occasional modernistic updates. The Rangers received their franchise from the National Hockey League on May 15, 1926, and began play on November 16, 1926, with a 1-0 victory over the Montreal Maroons.

THE RANGERS' PAPA. George L. "Tex" Rickard was a boxing man really, and he knew next to nothing about hockey, except that it was great at the box office. When he brought a hockey team to New York in 1926, the press called the club "Tex's Rangers," and the latter part of the name has been with us for 78 years. Their other nickname, the "Broadway Blueshirts," has been around just as long.

THE FIRST GENERAL MANAGER. Connie Smythe, probably the most dapper man in hockey, complete with trademark top hat and tails, was the Rangers' first general manager. He assembled a talented and veteran team, but he lasted only three months on the job and was fired before the team's first season even began in 1926.

AN EARLY "HAT TRICK." In 1938, Smythe was running the Toronto Maple Leafs. He disagreed, obviously, with an official's call, and took matters, quite literally, into his own hands. The still present top hat went flying in the ensuing scuffle on Madison Square Garden ice. Rangers goalie Davey Kerr watched from a safe distance.

THE "SILVER FOX." Lester Patrick earned his nickname, the "Silver Fox," not only from his full shock of silver hair but also from his sagacity in all things relating to hockey. Lester ran the Rangers, either as coach or general manager, for 20 seasons (1926–1927 to 1945–1946), wading into the New York scene with great relish. "Lester didn't adjust to New York," quipped Tommy Gorman, boss of the rival New York Americans, "New York adjusted to him." Lester's sons, Lynn and Muzz, both starred for and coached the Rangers. The Patricks are known as hockey's "Royal Family."

THE "A LINE." They were, quite simply, the greatest line of their era. The "A Line" was made up of Frank Boucher at center between the Cook brothers, right wing Bill (on the left) and left wing Bun (on the right). The nickname came from the "A" Line subway that was being constructed, but not yet running beneath Eighth Avenue and the third Madison Square Garden in 1926. Legendary Canadian broadcaster Foster Hewitt said that the A Line "looked like they had the puck on a string." The two Cooks and Boucher all made the Hockey Hall of Fame.

LESTER PATRICK NIGHT. Following a season and a half in corporate limbo, but still carrying the symbolic title of vice president, Lester Patrick decided on retirement from the Rangers. On December 3, 1947, the Madison Square Garden Corporation held Lester Patrick Night, the very first "night" to honor a Rangers employee. The "A Line" was symbolically reunited and joined by two bruising defensemen from the Original Rangers. Pictured, from left to right, are Bun Cook, Ivan "Ching" Johnson, Bill Cook, Lester Patrick, Clarence "Taffy" Abel, and Frank Boucher.

PROCLAIMING LESTER. The city of New York delivered a special proclamation to honor Lester Patrick on his big night at the Garden. Beaming sons Muzz (on the left) and Lynn, both recently retired players, joined their dad for the festivities. The younger Patricks eventually followed in Lester's footsteps and coached the Blueshirts.

13

"IRON MAN" I. As a Ranger, Murray Murdoch never missed a game. He played in the team's first game on November 16, 1926, and in the next 562, for a total of 563 (including playoff games), making the solid left wing the NHL's first "Iron Man." He was the last surviving member of the Original Rangers, and at the time of his death on May 17, 2001, he was the oldest living former NHL player, at 96 years of age. The secret to his longevity? "Hockey," Murdoch would chuckle.

"GENTLEMAN FRANK." The center on the "A Line" was "Gentleman" Frank Boucher, one of the cleanest players of any era. Boucher won the Lady Byng Trophy so many times (seven) that the NHL gave it to him permanently and had a new trophy struck. Despite his roots in Ontario, Boucher became a New Yorker at heart. He stayed on the Manhattan scene for 30 seasons as a player, coach, and general manager.

A WINNING STREAK. The Rangers of 1939–1940, en route to their third Stanley Cup championship, whoop it up in their Madison Square Garden locker room in January 1940 after going 18 consecutive games without a defeat. The streak eventually stretched to 19 games, and it stands as a team record today. The Rangers won 14 games and tied five on the streak. Pictured in the center are, from left to right, Lester Patrick, Davey Kerr, and Frank Boucher.

STANLEY CUP NUMBER THREE. The Rangers of 1940 celebrated long and hard after winning their third Stanley Cup on Saturday, April 13, 1940. The party, in the Tudor Room of the Royal York Hotel in Toronto, lasted well into the morning of April 14. Lester Patrick (in the center) and his Madison Square Garden boss John Reed Kilpatrick (to the right of Patrick) sprung for champagne and everyone drank from the Stanley Cup. "It was the cheapest champagne they could find," defenseman Walter "Babe" Pratt often joked, "but it was the best stuff any of us had ever tasted." The presence of NHL president Frank Calder (with eyeglasses next to the Stanley Cup) made the party official.

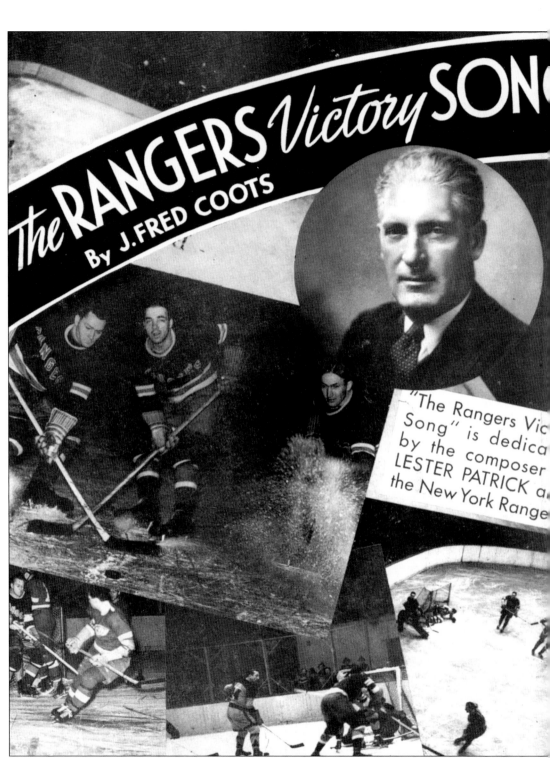

A LOVE LETTER ON ICE. In 1940, just after their Stanley Cup triumph, noted composer J. Fred Coots wrote "The Rangers Victory Song" and gifted the work to the Rangers and their general manager, Lester Patrick. When asked how many times she played the music, legendary organist

COOTS, composer of "The Rangers
Song" has a number of popular hits
credit, including "A Precious Little Thing
Love"—"Love Letters in the Sand" and
others. The Rangers express their thanks
Mr. Coots and to the American Society
Authors, Composers and Publishers for
proval of the gift of this song to the team.

Gladys Goodding said, "I can't count that high." Fans of a certain age can still whistle or hum Coots's lilting tune.

THE CHAMPS SCATTERED. Only a handful of the championship 1940 Rangers returned to New York to celebrate after winning the Stanley Cup in Toronto. Most of the players scattered to their permanent homes in Canada. The official team picture was a montage of player headshots composed in a Manhattan photograph studio.

THE GAME WINNER. Bryan Hextall, a left-handed shooting right wing, scored the goal that won the 1940 Cup for the Rangers. Hextall's winning shot was a hard backhander that beat Toronto netminder Turk Broda high on the right side. Suddenly, the Rangers were hugging and hollering. The Stanley Cup was theirs for a third time. As was commonplace at the time, Hextall did not return to New York to celebrate and instead went to his home in Manitoba.

THE "BREAD LINE." The Rangers' top line of 1940, the "Bread Line," was so named because it was the team's bread and butter. It featured, from left to right, Mac Colville (right wing), his brother Neil Colville (center), and Alex Shibicky (left wing). They were the youngest line in the NHL at the time, and the trio was also known as the "Stream-Line." Coach Frank Boucher called the Colvilles and Shibicky "Prairie Boys," as all three hailed from western Canada.

"CHING, CHING CHINAMAN." Although he finished his career with the hated Americans, Ivan "Ching" Johnson was one of the most beloved of the Original Rangers, a darling with the fans. "Ching, Ching Chinaman," they would yell. A fierce open-ice bodychecker, Johnson was injury prone, but he played on anyway. "Hey, it's what I do," he would explain. "I recover in the summer." His wide grin and gleaming bald pate were a fixture at Madison Square Garden for 11 seasons with the Rangers and one with the Americans.

BROTHER "BUN." Cook's real first name was Fred. He was Bill's brother and the left wing on the "A Line." His nickname, "Bun" or "Bunny," owed its birth to his habit of hopping on his skates like a bunny to gain momentum. He played 10 seasons in New York and won two Stanley Cups before being sold to the Boston Bruins in 1936.

"MR. FIRST." Bill Cook was the Rangers' first captain. He took the team's first two faceoffs (one ceremonial and one real) and scored the club's first goal, the game winner in the Rangers' very first game. He was arguably the best player of his era and is the only man in Rangers history to be presented with two Stanley Cups. He is shown here being honored by broadcaster Bill Chadwick and the Rangers Alumni Association in 1986. When Gordie Howe came into the NHL in 1946, some old-timers said, "There's the next Bill Cook." That says something.

AND "MR. LAST." Forty-two years later, Cook also did the honors for the ceremonial "last" goal at the third Madison Square Garden on February 11, 1968. He glided toward the empty Eighth Avenue net and slid the puck into it. The legendary organist Gladys Goodding played "Auld Lang Syne." Cook was extremely emotional afterward. "So many of my memories are in these walls," he said.

21

BURCHARD'S ODE. The most famous poem in Rangers history, "An Ode to Lester's Gallant Stand," was penned by sportswriter Jim Burchard of the *New York World-Telegram*. It was a tribute to Lester Patrick, who at 44 years of age, stood in as goalie and saved a Stanley Cup playoff game in 1928. This is Burchard's original manuscript, composed with precious few edits on a manual typewriter.

LESTER DONS THE PADS. This photograph of Lester Patrick as a goaltender was taken after his heroic stand in the 1928 Stanley Cup playoffs. The dramatic effect of Patrick's fete only grew as the years went by. Patrick played some goal as a youngster, and he regularly did so in practice during the 1920s. Lester also played a single game on defense with the Rangers of 1926–1927.

HOLLYWOOD PHIL. In the early 1940s, Metro-Goldwyn-Mayer was planning a hockey movie called *The Great Canadian*, starring Clark Gable and Myrna Loy. The Rangers were recruited for some of the skating scenes. Fiery Phil Watson was Gable's stand-in, and he even began growing a pencil mustache. The movie was never made. Watson went on to win a Stanley Cup with the Montreal Canadiens.

PEPPERPOT PHIL. As a player, Watson was a scrappy center who could also play right wing. He played 12 seasons in New York and later coached the team as well. In 1943–1944, thinking that wartime restrictions would prohibit Watson from crossing between Canada and the United States, the Rangers "loaned" Watson to the Montreal Canadiens, and the Canadiens promptly won the Stanley Cup.

MADISON SQUARE GARDEN CORPORATION

49TH AND 50TH STREETS-EIGHTH AVENUE

NEW YORK

EXECUTIVE OFFICES: 307 WEST 49TH STREET

LESTER PATRICK
VICE PRESIDENT

April 30, 1940

Dear Clint:

You will find enclosed herewith checks covering your share of the playoffs, viz:

Canadian Funds - $ 377.62
American Funds -   636.60

It is needless for me to tell you how sincerely I appreciate your efforts during the past season to attain our objective of winning the Stanley Cup. However, I wished to go further than mere words and was anxious to show this appreciation in a more material and substantial manner. With this thought in mind, I approached Colonel Kilpatrick and recommended that each player be given a bonus from the Corporation of Five Hundred Dollars. I am sure that you will be delighted to learn that Colonel Kilpatrick heartily and enthusiastically approved. The check is enclosed herewith.

Wishing you a very pleasant and happy summer,

Sincerely,

Lester Patrick

Encl.
LP az

Mr. Clint Smith
Box 382
Kamsack, Sask.
Canada

THANKS, FELLAS. By today's standards, it was a monetary pittance. "But to us, it was a mountain, a big mountain," recalled speedy center Clint Smith. He was one of 15 members of the 1939–1940 Rangers who got three checks totaling $1,514.22 just two and a half weeks after winning a third Stanley Cup on April 13, 1940. "We didn't spend them fast," said Smith. "I can tell you that much."

Two

THE WORLD'S MOST FAMOUS ARENA

THE "OLD GARDEN." Madison Square Garden number three, complete with its ornate marquee known throughout the world, quickly became a New York institution that lasted for 42 years. It served the city with the widest possible array of sporting events, cultural attractions, and trade and family shows. Pulitzer Prize–winning sportswriter Red Smith called it "simply the most famous and glamorous arena in creation."

MSG III. Built in just 249 days at a cost of $5.6 million, the third Madison Square Garden opened its doors with a six-day bike race on November 28, 1925. This rare interior view of the "house that Tex built" under construction shows the Ninth Avenue end of the new building. With its steeply sloped seating area, the Garden was built primarily for boxing but was an excellent hockey venue as well. The Rangers made their debut in their new digs on November 16, 1926, with a 1-0 victory over the Montreal Maroons.

UNDER CONSTRUCTION. This is an exterior view looking west on 49th Street as Madison Square Garden number three nears completion. The construction entrance can be seen at the far right facing Eighth Avenue, the approximate spot where MSG's new lobby would be. Polyclinic Hospital is in the background on 50th Street.

ST. NICK'S. Although they rarely played in Madison Square Garden (for much of their existence, they had their own rink at 66th Street and Columbus Avenue), the St. Nicholas Hockey Club, far better known simply as the St. Nick's, is a great part of the amateur hockey tradition in New York. The St. Nick's were formed in 1896, 30 years before the debut of the professional game in New York. They are still in operation today.

ONE WE MISSED. The greatest amateur hockey player never to play in Madison Square Garden was Hobart Amory Hare Baker. Known as Hobey, he starred at St. Paul's School in Concord, New Hampshire. Later, at Princeton, he captained the hockey team and the football team. They called him the "King of Hockey." He also played for the St. Nick's. A prominent pilot in his time, Hobey served in World War I and was killed flying his own plane on December 21, 1918. College hockey's highest honor, the Hobey Baker Award, is named in his memory.

AMATEUR HOCKEY

TRIPLEHEADERS. Amateur hockey, specifically the Metropolitan League, was a great Madison Square Garden tradition. Games were usually on Sunday afternoons in the 1940s and 1950s. A Met League game was followed by the semiprofessional New York Rovers. The NHL Rangers played at night. Many fans attended all three games. This particular program, from December 26, 1948, is historic. It features the Sherbrooke Red Raiders, who had an all-black forward line consisting of left wing Manny McIntyre and brothers center Herbie Carnegie and right wing Ossie Carnegie. This was the first appearance ever of a black hockey player at Madison Square Garden. (Photograph courtesy of Don O'Hanley Collection.)

MAYBE YES, MAYBE NO. Was there really a "curse" on the Rangers, one that prevented them from winning a Stanley Cup for 54 years between 1940 and 1994? Some say yes and attribute the bad fortune to Madison Square Garden executives, led by president John Reed Kilpatrick, who burned the Garden's mortgage in the hallowed Stanley Cup. That was in February 1941, less than a year after the Rangers had won the championship. Others say no; the curse was just an unfortunate run in team history.

FAREWELL. The six living members of the Original Rangers of 1926 salute the crowd at the closing ceremonies of MSG III on Sunday afternoon, February 11, 1968. They are, from left to right, Bun Cook, Bill Cook, Ching Johnson, Butch Keeling, Frank Boucher, and Murray Murdoch. That evening, the six journeyed 16 blocks south to attend the opening of MSG IV, a gala entertainment spectacular that featured Bob Hope and Bing Crosby.

HE IS MAD. College hockey was a staple at both Madison Square Gardens, particularly in the 1960s and 1970s, when the Garden promoted the ECAC Holiday Hockey Festival. Teams such as Clarkson, St. Lawrence, Harvard, Yale, Brown, Providence, Northeastern, Bowdoin, and others appeared regularly. This Clarkson defenseman is none too happy about missing an open net.

"KING" FOR A DAY. Right wing Larry "King" Kwong is the only player of Chinese descent ever to play for the Rangers. It was only for a single game in 1947–1948, but the appearance was unique. (Photograph courtesy of Don O'Hanley Collection.)

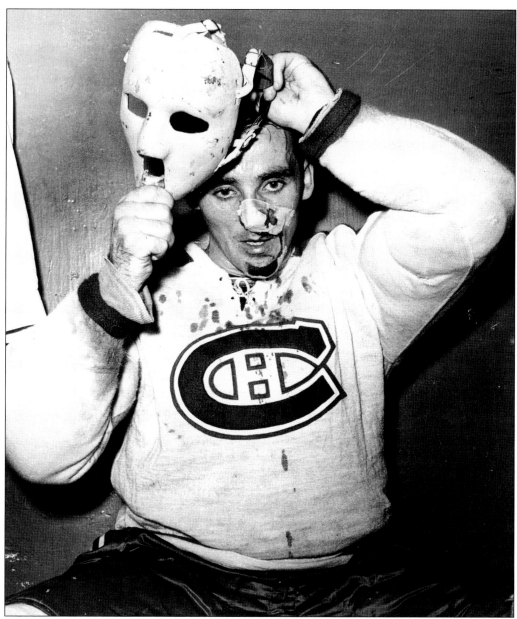

HOCKEY HISTORY IS MADE. The very face of hockey changed at Madison Square Garden on the night of November 1, 1959. Montreal goalie Jacques Plante became the first NHL goalie to wear a mask in a game. Plante suffered a severe cut when he was hit by a sharp backhander off the stick of the Rangers' captain and ace right wing, Andy Bathgate. He returned to the ice and snapped on a sand-colored mask. Thanks to Plante, the mask was here to stay, and goalies throughout the NHL quickly donned facial protection.

WHAT IS THIS? For several games during the 1965–1966 season, Madison Square Garden painted its hockey boards half red. It was an experiment for television to see whether the puck would be more distinguishable than with white boards. It was not. In this photograph, left wing Vic Hadfield checks Chicago defenseman Pat Stapleton while Jean Ratelle fishes for the puck.

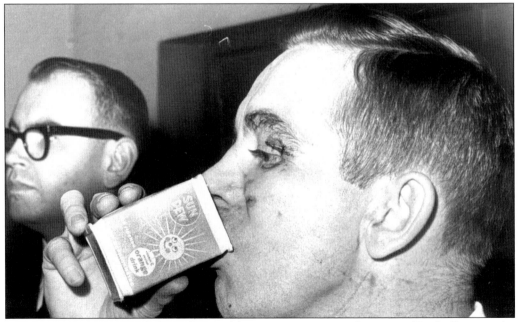

"CAT" CLAWED. He needed stitches and he was not even in the game! Emile Francis, the Rangers general manager, went to question goal judge Arthur Reichert's call in a game against the Detroit Red Wings on November 21, 1965. A melee broke out with a bunch of fans, and many of the Rangers scaled the 10-foot end glass to help "the Cat." It was one of the most memorable scenes in MSG history and made the front pages of the next day's newspapers.

AULD LANG SYNE. Closing day for Madison Square Garden number three came on the afternoon of February 11, 1968. Sixty-two former NHL All-Stars clad in their uniforms circled the ice again and again. At the time, it was the greatest collection of NHL talent ever in one building. Dewy-eyed fans showered the players with thunderous applause. The final game was a 3-3 tie with the Detroit Red Wings. (Photograph by Barton Silverman.)

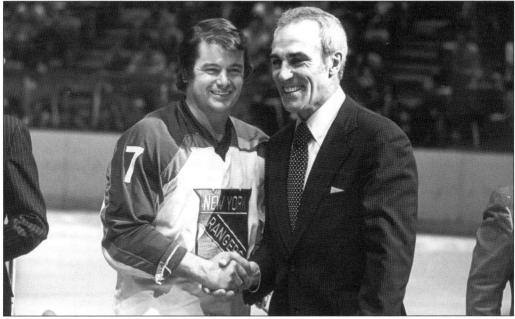

DURABLE BUDDIES. In this photograph, Harry Howell (1,160 games), pictured on the right, congratulates Rod Gilbert (1,065 games) on the occasion of Rod Gilbert Night, March 9, 1977. They are two of the most recognizable and most durable players in Rangers history. Between them, they played 2,225 games as Rangers. Brian Leetch has since surpassed Gilbert with the second most games played in team history.

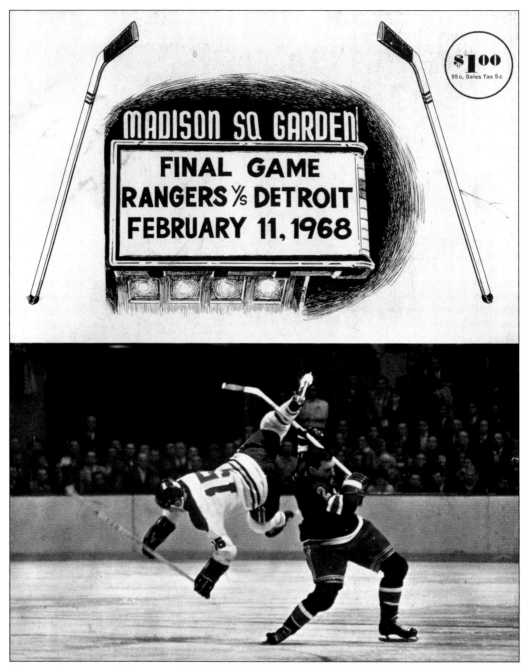

SAYING GOODBYE. The program for the final game at MSG III featured a drawing of the old Garden marquee by artist Charlie McGill and a Barton Silverman photograph of Rangers defenseman Wayne Hillman flipping Montreal Canadiens right wing Bobby Rousseau.

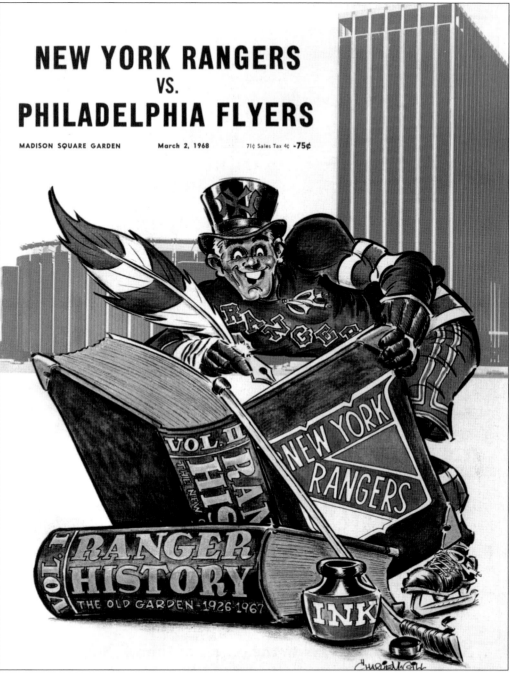

NEW YORK RANGERS
VS.
PHILADELPHIA FLYERS

MADISON SQUARE GARDEN   March 2, 1968   71¢ Sales Tax 4¢ **-75¢**

SAYING HELLO. Another Charlie McGill program cover was on tap for the hockey opening of MSG IV on February 18, 1968. A top-hatted historian prepared to write all the new events and happenings in the Rangers' new home. The Rangers won their opener over the Philadelphia Flyers 3-1.

THE LAST. The honor of scoring the last real goal in Madison Square Garden number three went to Rangers center Jean Ratelle, who slipped the puck past Detroit Red Wings goalie Roger Crozier, the final goal of a 3-3 tie. The Garden's customary sellout crowd of 15,925 was on hand to witness. (Photograph by Barton Silverman.)

AND THE FIRST. One week later, right wing Wayne Hicks of the Philadelphia Flyers, wearing a white uniform on the right, scored the first goal in the new Garden, deflecting a shot past Eddie Giacomin of the Rangers. Later in the game, center Phil Goyette scored the Rangers' first goal in their new home. (Photograph by Barton Silverman.)

A New York Institution. Still on Eighth Avenue, but on the east side instead of the west, and 16 blocks south of its predecessor, the fourth Madison Square Garden stands majestically, not far from another New York City landmark, the Empire State Building. The MSG complex reaches from Eighth Avenue to Seventh and spans 31st Street to 33rd Street.

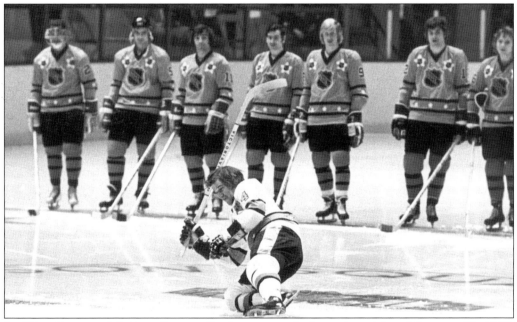

It Was Staged. Madison Square Garden was packed on the night of January 30, 1973, with a crowd of 16,986, an All-Star Game record at the time. The fans booed lustily at each introduction of a member of the Boston Bruins, who had beaten the Rangers in the Stanley Cup finals just eight months earlier. They cheered when superstar Bobby Orr took a carefully planned pratfall at center ice during the pregame introductions.

CLEANING UP. Before any Zambonis cleaned the Madison Square Garden ice, that chore was accomplished by two large barrels that were filled with hot water. After the ice was scraped to remove shavings, the barrels were pushed by Garden workmen, and presto, there was a fresh sheet of ice for the next period of play.

"CHIEF" I. He was hardly a track star, but for approximately 15 seasons (*c.* 1970 to 1985), Bob Comas of Brooklyn was fast friends with the Ranger faithful. Clad in a sometimes ratty Indian headdress and a Rangers jersey, he entertained the fans with lope-like jogs around the Garden's various levels, usually with arms upraised. When his legs started to go, he simply walked and the fans sometimes showered him with debris. "It was devastating," Comas recalled. "I really thought I was the 'People's Chief.'"

"Veteran" Rangers. Three of the youngest "old Rangers" at the closing of the third Garden were defenseman Harry Howell, right wing Andy Bathgate, and defenseman Bill Gadsby. Between them, the veteran trio combined for 2,236 games as Rangers. Howell is the team's all-time leader in games played.

It Is Over. Madison Square Garden was crackling with fireworks and applause as the Rangers iced their fourth Stanley Cup on June 14, 1994. The clock reads, "0:00," and the Rangers celebrate in a tight knot on the far right, while the Vancouver Canucks (on the left along the boards) experience the agony of defeat. (Photograph by George Kalinsky.)

MSG's Best. Inarguably, at least in the minds of most hockey fans, Wayne Gretzky and Vladislav Tretiak are the two greatest hockey players ever to compete at Madison Square Garden. The two megastars met many times in various international competitions, but their paths never crossed at the World's Most Famous Arena. New York's hockey fans are undoubtedly poorer for that.

Three

THE COACHES:
BEHIND THE BENCH

DOUBLE DUTY. Four different men named Patrick have coached the Rangers: Lester, sons Lynn and Muzz, and grandson Craig. Muzz, shown here in a classic publicity photograph pose, did it twice, and not too successfully.

A TRUE PIONEER. For 13 seasons, from 1926–1927 through 1938–1939, Lester Patrick was the only coach the Rangers knew. He worked 604 games (second only to Emile Francis with 654), won two Stanley Cups, and worked heroically to make the game of hockey a success in New York City.

SECOND UP. Following a brilliant playing career, Frank Boucher became the Rangers' second head coach, succeeding Lester Patrick in 1939–1940. He won the Stanley Cup in his first season behind the bench, 1939–1940, but it was downhill from there on. Boucher finished his coaching career with 181 wins and 263 defeats. As a player, coach, and general manager, Boucher was on the New York hockey scene for 30 years.

LYNN'S MAGIC. He was only at it for a season and a half, but Lynn Patrick, the Rangers' third coach, guided the team all the way to the Stanley Cup finals in 1949–1950. They lost in a seven-game final-round series to the Detroit Red Wings. Following the season, in a surprise move, Patrick bolted to coach the rival Boston Bruins. Here, Patrick discusses his team's prospects with sportswriter Dana Mozley of the *New York Daily News*.

A BENCH DUD. As great as he was as a player, and he may have been the very best of his era, Bill Cook was a dud as the coach of the Rangers for a season and a half, starting midway through the 1951–1952 season. With just 34 victories in 117 games, he was promptly replaced by general manager Frank Boucher for the start of the 1953–1954 season. For the record, Boucher did not fare much better in the 39 games he stayed behind the bench.

A GOOD SKATE. Some said Alfie Pike was simply "too nice a guy to be a coach." Others said he "lacked passion" and "couldn't fire up a furnace." His record supported all three comments. A winning percentage of only .378 ranks Pike the lowest of any Ranger coach who worked more than one season. As a player—and a rookie at that—he won a Stanley Cup in 1940.

"Sully" Stumbled. Despite his nickname, dapper George "Red" Sullivan definitely bled Rangers blue, and he most certainly loved his time in the Big Apple. A popular sparkplug center as a player, he made the playoffs five times (twice with the Rangers). As a coach, he was not nearly as lucky. He never made the playoffs and had a weak .385 winning percentage, one of the worst in team history.

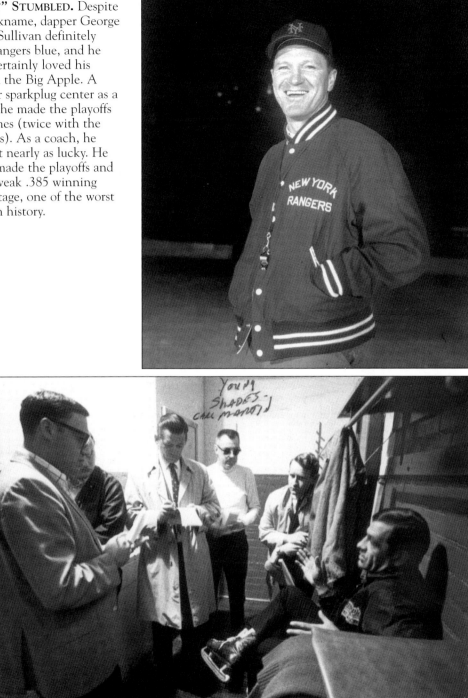

"Boomer" Speaks. Bernie "Boom Boom" Geoffrion was never at a loss for words during his abbreviated term as coach of the Rangers in 1968–1969. Despite a solid 22-18-3 record, Geoffrion was troubled by an ulcer and replaced by Emile Francis on January 17, 1969. Boom Boom later coached the Atlanta Flames and the Montreal Canadiens.

"THE CAT" SPARKLED. Whenever the Rangers of his era (1965–1975) needed a spark of energy, Emile "the Cat" Francis was ready at the switch. Three different times he went behind the bench, and his teams responded. "He was strict, but he was fair, always fair," remembered center Walt Tkaczuk. The Cat's coaching record was more than fair: 342 wins and a .602 winning percentage.

SAVVY "STEWIE." Ron Stewart was a Ranger for 306 games in two different shifts, and Emile Francis turned to him to become the Rangers' 14th head coach on May 19, 1975. "Stewie" lasted only 39 games and stumbled to a 15-20-4 record before new general manager John Ferguson took over halfway through the 1975–1976 season.

FERGY THE FIRST. When John Ferguson became the Rangers' 15th coach on January 7, 1976, he was the first non-Ranger to hold the position. All of his 14 predecessors, from Lester Patrick to Ron Stewart, had also played for the team. Fergy stumbled to a 43-59-19 record and quickly handed the coaching reins to his old Montreal buddy Jean-Guy Talbot for the 1977–1978 season.

ONLY LOGICAL. "Hey, coaches sweat too," reasoned former defenseman Jean-Guy Talbot when he showed up wearing a sweat suit behind the Rangers' bench in 1977–1978, the very first NHL coach to don casual wear on the job. He did not sweat that much, though, posting only 30 wins in 80 games before ceding the coaching reins to Fred Shero on June 2, 1978.

GETTING THEIR ATTENTION. Talbot might have worn a sweat suit, but no Ranger coach in 78 seasons ever had to go to the lengths that Red Kelly of the Toronto Maple Leafs did in 1975. Kelly coached a game at Madison Square Garden with a bullwhip in his hand. It did not work, and the Rangers beat the Leafs 4-1.

"THE FOG." It was the aptest of nicknames, Freddie Shero's was, and "the Fog" was often a thick one. His tinted glasses gave him a mysterious look. He often talked in parables, and his habit of mispronouncing names was maddening to many. Still, the Fog got results and spirited the Rangers to the Stanley Cup finals in 1979. He won more games than he lost and said, "Isn't that what I'm supposed to do?"

VENUES FOR CHANGE. From c. 1969 to 1980, the Rangers usually used two dining facilities within Madison Square Garden, the Penn Plaza Club and the Hall of Fame, to announce their coaching changes. "Where coaches go to die," is what sportswriter Bob Gockley of the *Long Island Press* called the two eateries. Here, Larry Popein is named the Rangers' 13th coach on June 4, 1973, and is interviewed by football-legend-turned-sportscaster Frank Gifford. He lasted a mere 41 games.

HERB'S WAY. From the 1981–1982 season until halfway through 1984–1985, Herb Brooks proved he could do with the pros what he had done with the 1980 U.S. Olympians, the "Miracle on Ice" boys. "Good enough is not good enough" was a favorite mantra of his. His Rangers were good enough to post a 131-113-41 record on his watch and make the playoffs every season, but they never won the Stanley Cup.

SMILES TO FROWNS. Rangers general manager Phil Esposito (on the left) and coach Michel Bergeron (on the right) were all smiles presenting a sculpture on Eddie Giacomin Night, March 15, 1989. Fifteen days later, on April Fool's Day, Esposito fired Bergeron and took the coaching reins himself. It did not work. Esposito lost the final two games of the season and four straight playoff games to the Pittsburgh Penguins.

WELL TRAVELED. Roger Neilson is one of the most well-traveled coaches in the history of the National Hockey League. His .566 winning percentage in four and a half seasons is third in team annals, trailing only Mike Keenan and Emile Francis. Neilson, who pioneered the use of video technology in the NHL, was also well known for his large variety of garish neckties.

Four

THE GOALIE GANG

SOLID IN GOAL. Old-time Rangers fans will tell you that Chuck "Bonnie Prince Charlie" Rayner was the most valuable Ranger of his era. Rayner led the Rangers to within a goal of the Stanley Cup in 1950 and won the Hart Trophy that year as the NHL's most valuable player. Rayner played 10 seasons in New York, two of them with the Rangers' archrivals, the Americans.

DAVEY DOES IT. For most of their first eight seasons, the Rangers had three goalies—Lorne Chabot, John Ross Roach, and Andy Aitkenhead. Once Davey Kerr arrived in 1934–1935, the job was his for the next seven years. Kerr rarely missed a game. He won a Vezina Trophy and a Stanley Cup in 1939–1940 and posted 47 shutouts, including seven in the Stanley Cup playoffs. Here Davey deflects a backhander off the stick of Boston's ace center Milt Schmidt.

ALMOST EVERYTHING WENT IN. The great Jacques Plante was only a Ranger for a season and a half in the mid-1960s, but he was the goalie when this prizewinning photograph was snapped at Madison Square Garden. The puck, Plante's stick, his glove, and even a sliding Lowell MacDonald ended up in the net. Defenseman Rod Seiling (No. 16) did not. Plante, primarily on the basis of his play with the Montreal Canadiens, made it to the Hockey Hall of Fame.

THE OLYMPIC GOALIE WAS DECKED.
Goalie Jack McCartan, less than
two weeks after backstopping the
U.S. Olympic team to a gold medal
in Squaw Valley, California, made
his National Hockey League debut
against the Chicago Blackhawks at
Madison Square Garden on March
9, 1960. Reggie Fleming of the
Blackhawks (No. 6) made McCartan's
debut a rough one, slugging the
netminder near the Rangers' blue
line. The game ended in a 1-1 tie.

JACQUES AND GILLES. Inimitable goaltender Jacques Plante was always a perfectionist and a great instructor who loved to share his knowledge with just about anyone who would listen. Here the future Hall of Famer imparts some words of wisdom to young netminder Gilles Villemure at Ranger training camp in Winnipeg in 1964.

GUMP AND JACK. Veteran Gump Worsley shares some pointers with rookie goalie Jack McCartan at a Rangers practice session in 1960. McCartan, who won a gold medal with the 1960 U.S. Olympic team, played only 12 games with the Rangers before embarking on a long career in the minors.

GIACOMIN GRAPPLES. Eddie Giacomin and Bernie Parent decidedly did not see eye to eye in this 1971 tussle between the Rangers and the Toronto Maple Leafs. Parent's mask was eventually ripped off and thrown into the crowd by fun-loving Vic Hadfield. The mask, Parent's only one, quickly made its way up to the blue seats with Toronto's assistant general manager "King" Clancy in hot pursuit. He never caught up with it. A couple of days went by, and the mask was returned anonymously.

NEEDLING JACQUES. Eddie Giacomin was never one for gamesmanship, but he made an exception on November 22, 1969, when he recorded his 26th shutout. As he left the ice, Giacomin threw his arms into the air a la Jacques Plante, his opponent in St. Louis that evening. Plante was the first goalie to signal victory with arms upraised.

NOT HAPPY. Clearly, Rangers fans were not too happy with the waiver deal that sent Eddie Giacomin to the Detroit Red Wings on October 31, 1975. A day earlier, the Rangers traded Derek "the Turk" Sanderson to the St. Louis Blues. That one was not too popular either. Signs of any kind were soon banned at the Garden—a fire hazard the security folks said.

TO THE ROOF. Eventually, goalie Eddie Giacomin's familiar No. 1 made it to the rafters of Madison Square Garden, where it joined the equally familiar No. 7 of Rod Gilbert. "What a feeling that was," said Giacomin. "I will never forget it." Aside from Wayne Gretzky's No. 99, which has been retired league-wide, Giacomin's and Gilbert's remain the only New York numbers to be taken out of circulation. (Photograph by George Kalinsky.)

GOALIE GREATS. Aside from more modern-day greats such as John Vanbiesbrouck and Mike Richter, these are the most famous goaltenders in Rangers history. They are, from left to right, Chuck Rayner, Lorne "Gump" Worsley, Gilles Villemure, and Eddie Giacomin. The occasion was Eddie Giacomin Night on March 15, 1989. Rayner won the Hart Trophy as the NHL's MVP in 1950.

ACE GOALIES. They both played just over 10 seasons in New York, and they both won a Vezina Trophy. John Vanbiesbrouck (No. 34) presents a miniature Vezina Trophy to Eddie Giacomin in 1989. Vanbiesbrouck won his Vezina in 1985–1986, while Giacomin shared his Vezina with Gilles Villemure in 1970–1971.

OUTSPOKEN GOALIE. At the very top of the list of unique characters who have worn the Rangers uniform for 78 seasons is the name of Lorne John "Gump" Worsley, the quotable and lovable goalkeeper who played 10 seasons in the Big Apple from 1953 to 1963. Worsley baited coaches, particularly Phil Watson. "As a coach, he was a good waiter," Worsley said of Watson, one of the many salvos the two exchanged throughout the length of their fractious relationship. Yet the fans loved "the Gumper," admired his courage, and appreciated his wit. Worsley worked 583 games (all without a facemask) for New York. "My face is my mask," he was fond of saying. This picture is from 1959.

GILLES AT THE TOP. It is one of the least known—and most remarkable—statistics in Rangers history. With an overall record of 98 wins against 54 defeats, goaltender Gilles Villemure has a .645 winning percentage, by far the best of any of the more than 70 men who have tended goal for the Blueshirts. He also won a Vezina Trophy with Eddie Giacomin in 1971. Villemure played half of the 26th NHL All-Star Game at Madison Square Garden.

Five

THE NEW YORK RANGERS: NATIVE AND ADOPTED SONS

IT IS HIS TURF. Very few people have done as much for hockey in New York City as native New Yorker Brian Mullen, shown here amidst a bunch of New York kids who no doubt grew up much like Mullen himself. This photograph was taken at Hell's Kitchen Park on 48th Street and 10th Avenue. Mullen played for both the Rangers and the Islanders during the course of his 11-year NHL career.

ANOTHER RANGERS FIRST. In 1947, the Rangers produced the very first NHL team press guide, or yearbook, a painstaking research effort by native New Yorker and hockey historian Stan Saplin, who was then the team's publicity director. Saplin's love for the game—and for the Rangers—was unsurpassed.

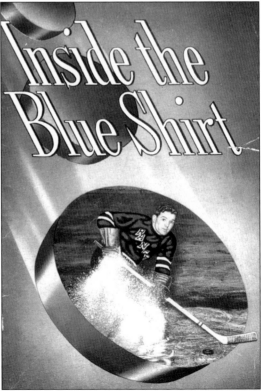

VOLUME II. In 1948, Saplin changed the name of his work to *Inside the Blueshirt*, adding new features and continuing to spin the Rangers' legend and lore. Clarence Campbell, the new president of the National Hockey League, had high praise for *Inside the Blueshirt*, calling it "a superlative pioneering effort in the field of hockey literature."

THREE FOR NEW YORK. It was only fitting that New York City native Brian Mullen chose Madison Square Garden to score the only hat trick of his 11-year National Hockey League career. The date was October 19, 1988, a 5-1 Rangers victory over the Washington Capitals. Mullen's postgame smile lit up the MSG dressing room where he served earlier for several seasons as a Rangers stickboy. Brian and his brother Joe, born and raised on West 49th Street just down the block from MSG number three, are the highest-scoring United States–born brother combination in the history of the NHL.

TWO FOR NEW YORK. Brooklyn-born talk show giant Larry King, a Rangers fan from the 1940s, had the honor of presenting longtime Rangers general manager and coach Emile Francis with the Lester Patrick Award in 1982. The award, for "outstanding service to hockey in the United States," was presented in Washington, D.C., which Francis regretted. "I wished it could have been in New York," he said. "That's my adopted home town, and always will be."

VOICES OF NEW YORK. For eight seasons from 1973–1974 to 1980–1981, native New Yorkers Jim Gordon (on the left) and Bill "the Big Whistle" Chadwick were partners on the telecasts of the New York Rangers. They were, in some quarters at least, as popular as the players they covered. This photograph in Madison Square Garden was taken prior to their last regular-season home game on April 3, 1981, a 3-1 victory over the Chicago Blackhawks. "I worked with lots and lots of people in my time," Gordon recalled, "but Bill Chadwick was the only 'partner' I ever had." Chadwick came to the broadcast booth following a sterling career as an NHL referee.

"THE BIG WHISTLE." As a kid growing up in Jamaica, Queens, Bill Chadwick was known as "Buster." Among his many teams was the Floral Park Hockey Club. Prior to his storied broadcasting career, where he earned the nickname "the Big Whistle," Chadwick had an even more storied career as an NHL referee. That landed him in the Hockey Hall of Fame.

WESTSIDERS. Raised on West 49th Street, just a slap shot away from the third Madison Square Garden, Brian Mullen (on the right) and his brother Joe both became NHL stars. They played against each other, Brian for the Wales Conference and Joe for the Campbell Conference, in the 40th NHL All-Star Game at Edmonton on February 7, 1989.

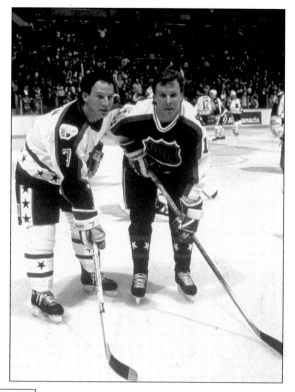

NEW YORK, NEW YORK. Brian and his brother Joe became the highest-scoring United States–born brother combination in NHL history. Along the way, Brian met many famous New Yorkers, such as Gov. Mario Cuomo. Following his playing career, Brian worked in fan development with the NHL and later as radio analyst for his old team, the Rangers.

CONCRETE RANGERS. The World's Fair came to New York in 1964. Upcoming Ranger star Rod Gilbert (on the left), coach Red Sullivan (in the center), and veteran defenseman Harry Howell got their signatures and hand prints cast in concrete in front of the Schaefer Center in Flushing Meadow. Schaefer beer was a major sponsor of the Rangers—and the Garden—for many years.

THEY DID NOT. In 1974, the Rangers were battling the rival Philadelphia Flyers in a bitter Stanley Cup semifinal series. New York City was awash with playoff fever. Someone, either the cigarette company or the sign company, took it a step further on the Brooklyn-Queens Expressway, exhorting the Rangers to win. They did not. Philadelphia prevailed, four games to three, and went on to win the Stanley Cup.

NICKY RUMBLED. Native New Yorker Nick Fotiu was born on Staten Island. He had two tours of duty with the Rangers covering 455 games and a hefty 970 minutes in the penalty box. The big left wing was known mostly for his fighting ability, but he was a speedy skater and had a dangerously sneaky wrist shot that found its mark 41 times.

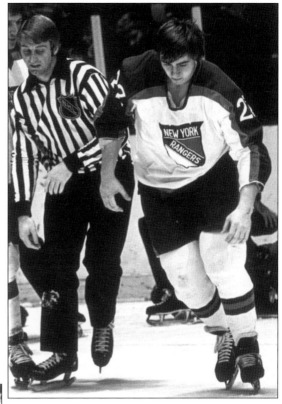

AND NICKY GAVE. Much to the consternation of his coaches—not to mention Garden security types and lawyers—Fotiu persisted with his habit of firing pucks high up toward the rafters before games. It was his way of giving back and seeing that a "blue seater" got a bonus. Between his playing style and his puck throwing, Fotiu was much adored by the fans. To be sure, the feeling was mutual.

CHRISTMAS AT THE GARDEN. Pop Marv Albert (in the center) and one-skated toddler Kenny Albert pay a visit to Santa Claus during a Rangers Christmas party on MSG ice in December 1969. Santa (actually Rangers staffer Paul Kanow) was good to Kenny. He grew up to be a top-flight sportscaster just like his dad.

TIMES CHANGE. Nearly 27 years later, in 1996, dad Marv and son Kenny went the formal route—complete with microphones—on the occasion of Kenny's wedding in New Jersey on August 10, 1996. Between the two of them, Marv and Kenny have lent the Albert name and, more importantly, the Albert voice to Rangers events for almost 40 years.

THE "MAVEN." If New York City hockey can be said to have a "soul," its name would be Stan Fischler. The Brooklyn-born "Maven" has probably written and spoken more words on hockey than any other person in the world. He has authored more than 70 books on his favorite sport and delivered countless incisive, not to mention controversial, comments to the telecasts of the Rangers, Islanders, and Devils.

IT WILL HAPPEN SOMEDAY. A native New Yorker has never coached the Rangers—not yet anyway. Brooklyn native Lou Vairo might have been a candidate, but he has spent his career with USA Hockey, coaching National and Olympic teams. Frank Boucher, Emile Francis, and Rod Gilbert all considered themselves adopted sons of New York, but you can not change your birthplace.

"Red Light" Is Unique. In 78 years of Rangers history, no one has commented continuously on more Rangers games than Sal "Red Light" Messina. The nickname, which came from his longtime broadcast partner Marv Albert, was a friendly one and referred unfairly to ex-goalie Messina's penchant for giving up goals. A native New Yorker, Sal was in the Rangers broadcast booth for 30 seasons, starting in 1973, and still makes cameo appearances. "Red Light" continues to shine.

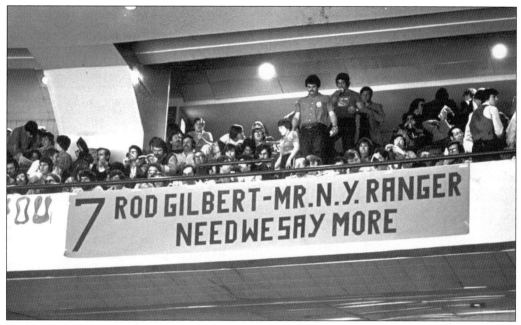

A Garden Salute. The sign said it all as the Rangers, players, and fans alike saluted Rod Gilbert, the team's all-time scoring leader and holder of most of its offensive scoring records, on March 9, 1977. From the blue seats (shown above) down to the reds, the fans gave Rod a rousing four-minute standing ovation. "It made my neck tingle," Rod recalled.

Searching for Words. When the big moment came and the spotlight ushered him onto the ice, Rod lost his speech, which he thought he had tucked into the left sleeve of his uniform. No. 7 was nervous, but he ad-libbed a perfect speech that thanked all the right people.

EPIC BATTLES. The New York Americans (wearing white jerseys) supplied the Rangers with their first bitter rivalry. The Amerks were co-tenants with the Blueshirts at Madison Square Garden, and the games between the two teams were fiercely fought and always sold out. The teams met 94 times between 1926–1927 and 1941–1942, when the Amerks folded. The

Rangers won 57 of the games, lost 23, and tied 14. This photograph is a specially posed "house portrait," with players and fans all facing the photographer at the Ninth Avenue end of the Garden. This game, which was played on November 15, 1936, celebrated the Rangers' 10th anniversary. The Rangers lost 2-1.

CITY KIDS. From its inception in 1987, the unique program called ICE HOCKEY in Harlem has benefited greatly from the charitable endeavors of the New York Rangers. Twice each season, the Rangers support the program's major fundraising events, and players regularly participate

72

in teaching clinics at various New York City locations. Ice Hockey in Harlem has helped thousands of underprivileged youngsters over the last 16 years.

Sports Illustrated

JANUARY 30, 1967   40 CENTS

NEW YORK'S
AMAZING RANGERS

TOP GOAL-GETTER ROD GILBERT

COVER BOY. On January 30, 1967, *Sports Illustrated* chose Rod Gilbert for its cover photograph. Gilbert became only the second Ranger to be so honored. Gilbert's idol, superstar right wing Andy Bathgate, was the first Ranger on a *Sports Illustrated* cover. "It was the first time I was ever in a professional photograph shoot," Gilbert recalled. "It took half a day for that one photograph."

Six

THE 1950S AND 1960S

THE "MIRACLE OF SQUAW VALLEY." Twenty years before the "Miracle of Lake Placid," the 1960 U.S. Olympic team captured a gold medal by defeating Czechoslovakia 9-4. Goalie Jack McCartan (in the center of the back row, partially obscured by stick) was quickly signed by the Rangers. The clinching game was played in the daytime in an open end arena. Two of the players wore black pitch under their eyes to reduce glare.

HISTORY REPEATS. Lynn Patrick, an All-Star left wing with the Rangers in 1942 and coach of the team that went to the Stanley Cup finals in 1950, tutors son Craig in 1955 at the Boston Garden. Twenty-five years later, the younger Patrick took over as general manager of the Rangers, succeeding grandfather Lester and uncle Muzz in the general manager's chair on November 21, 1980. Craig also coached the team, not once, but twice.

THE "ROCKET" GLARED. Among the greatest NHL stars to visit Madison Square Garden in the 1950s, none shone brighter than Maurice "Rocket" Richard of the Montreal Canadiens. The Rocket seemed to relish the New York stage and scored some of his biggest goals just off Broadway. Hard-hitting defenseman Bob Dill of the Rangers (No. 4) regularly tried to throw the Rocket off his game with open-ice bodychecks like this one.

ONE OF A KIND. For 31 years, 29 of them with the "big club," as he was fond of calling it, trainer Frank Paice was the Rangers' one constant. No one in team history worked more consecutive years in the same position as Frank Paice. He was more than just a trainer, serving at times as equipment manager, traveling secretary, confidante, and cheerleader. Paice is also the only trainer in NHL history to have his own hockey card (TOPPS, 1962–1963), assuring that his memory will never be forgotten, not only among his legion of friends but among hockey collectors as well.

HANDY ANDY. Ace right wing Andy Bathgate was the most popular Ranger of the 1950s, the team's first "superstar" as that word began to appear in the lexicon of all sports. He won the Hart Trophy as the NHL's most valuable player in 1959 and scored at least one goal in 10 consecutive games from December 15, 1962, to January 5, 1963. That is still a team record. "We really had some great talent on those teams [in the 1950s], but in my opinion, we didn't have the management team to put it together properly."

HONORING HARRY. On January 25, 1967, the Rangers made Harry Howell the very first player to receive a special night in his honor. Management, the players, and the fans showered the defenseman with a plethora of tributes and gifts. Years later, Rod Gilbert and Ed Giacomin, both former teammates of Howell, received similar nights. Harry's nickname was "the Horse." He played 1,160 games as a Ranger, the most in team history, all of them in venerable sweater No. 3.

GUMP'S DEBUT. Lorne "Gump" Worsley was only 20 years of age when he made his professional hockey debut as a member of the New York Rovers in 1949. He became one of the most beloved figures in Rangers history. He won the Calder Trophy as rookie of the year in 1952–1953. He also won four Stanley Cups and two Vezina trophies with the Montreal Canadiens. (Photograph courtesy of Don O'Hanley Collection.)

"IRON MAN" II. In reality, no one ever thought Murray Murdoch's streak of 563 consecutive games as a Ranger would ever be broken. But no one told that to Andy Hebenton, a plugging right wing who played 582 games without a miss from 1955 to 1963. Add in one season with the Boston Bruins and 10 more with Portland and Victoria of the Western League, and Hebenton played 1,062 professional games without a miss. Only the death of his father finally snapped the streak on October 18, 1967.

WHAT A DEAL. Winnipeg-born Monty Hall, far more famous as the host of television's popular *Let's Make a Deal* game show, was the color commentator-analyst for New York Rangers radio games in 1959–1960. "He said they paid him $50 a game," recalled play-by-play man Jim Gordon. "Not true, it was $35, same as me."

ONE FOR THE AGES. He never played for the Rangers, not for a minute, but in less than a minute—21 seconds to be exact—Bill "Wee Willie" Mosienko accomplished one of the most amazing feats in NHL history. The date was March 23, 1952. Mosienko scored three goals in 21 seconds in the third period, the last of the season for both the Rangers and the visiting Chicago Blackhawks. There were only 3,254 fans on hand, but according to one report, the fans cheered "with a volume that seemed to come from twice the number of throats when the record-breaking accomplishment was announced." The Blackhawks won 7-6.

THE LOYALISTS. From its inception in 1950, the New York Rangers Fan Club has been the most vocal and visible reminder of Rangers fans anywhere. The club celebrated its 50th anniversary in 2000. Over the years, its membership has fluctuated between 500 and 1,500 people, and many well-known celebrities have been among them. The club continues to flourish today.

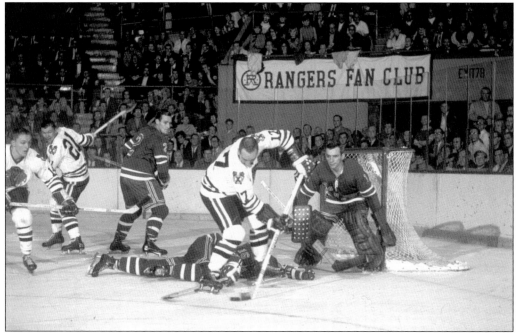

TRUE BLUE FANS. For many, many years, starting in the 1950s, the Rangers Fan Club banner was a regular sight hanging from the end promenade of MSG III. Rangers goalies, principally Chuck Rayner, Gump Worsley, and Eddie Giacomin (shown here), routinely waved to the loyal fans, usually during pregame warmups or at the end of a period. Rayner recalled, "It was a ritual, and easy. The same people were always in the same seats."

LOUIE TAKES A LICKING. It is probably the most celebrated—not to mention one-sided—fight in Rangers history. Immensely popular defenseman "Leaping" Lou Fontinato got his clock cleaned and his nose broken in this bloody battle at the Garden on February 1, 1959. Not even the officials, Art Skov (on the left) and Frank Udvari, cared to assess the damage to Fontinato's face. "Hey, we won the game," Fontinato would often say. (Photograph courtesy of Charlie Hoff.)

BLAZING THE TRAIL. Forget Thommie Bergman of Detroit, Borje Salming of Toronto, and Anders Hedberg and Ulf Nilsson of the Rangers. The very first Swedish-born player in the National Hockey League was left wing Ulf Sterner of the Rangers in 1964–1965. He played only four games before returning to his native Sweden.

FUTURE RANGERS. The New York Rovers team was a great part of the Rangers tradition, principally in the 1940s and 1950s. Rovers players, usually in their high teens or early twenties, learned the same system as the Rangers and were hopefully prepared if they got the call to join the Rangers.

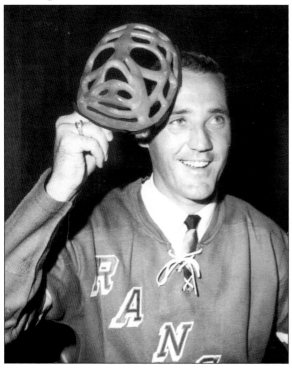

A SHOCKER. It was a shocking trade in the summer of 1963 when the Rangers acquired the great Jacques Plante from the Montreal Canadiens. It was Plante, four years earlier, who first introduced the facemask to the NHL. This photograph, from a press conference on July 29, 1963, shows Plante's second mask, not the one he wore on November 1, 1959.

Seven

UP FROM THE ASHES

THE GARDEN VOLCANO. Madison Square Garden erupted as only the Garden can when Peter Stemkowski scored his epic triple-overtime goal against the Chicago Blackhawks on April 29, 1971. It came at 1:29 of the third extra period, the fourth longest game in Rangers playoff history. "Believe me, I didn't even hear the cheering," Stemkowski said, "but some of the guys said it sounded like a volcano." (Photograph by Barton Silverman.)

"Chief" II. A popular Rangers defenseman for 12 seasons from 1962–1963 to 1973–1974, Jim "the Chief" Neilson was the Rangers' first player of North American Indian descent. He was part Danish and part Cree Indian. Neilson was such a strong skater that he was sometimes used as a left winger. Here, at the third Madison Square Garden, Neilson matches strides with Ron Stewart of the Boston Bruins. Stewart later played for and coached the Rangers.

Advantage Rangers. As shocking as it was, the blockbuster trade that sent captain Andy Bathgate to the Toronto Maple Leafs on February 22, 1964, brought a solid return to the Rangers. Right wing Bob Nevin captained the team for seven seasons and scored 168 goals and 342 points. He was also a terrific defensive asset.

ANOTHER ROD. Nineteen-year-old defenseman Rod Seiling was the youngest player in the Bathgate trade. He joined Rod Gilbert as the second Rod on the Rangers and patrolled the Rangers' blueline for 644 games over 10 seasons. In his first game as a Ranger, he slammed Chicago defenseman Pierre Pilote into the boards and immediately endeared himself to the Ranger faithful.

ARNIE ADDS. Much like Seiling, defenseman Arnie Brown was a solid, if unspectacular, producer from the Bathgate trade. "I had scouted those guys (Seiling and Brown) for more than a year," remembered general manager Emile Francis. "Believe me, I knew what kind of underwear they wore."

"MR. NEW YORK HOCKEY." Rod Gilbert's name has been synonymous with New York Rangers hockey for more than 40 seasons. He is the holder of virtually all of the team's offensive records and played the third most games (1,065) in team history. Gilbert also became the first member of the Rangers to make New York City his permanent home. Oft times during his career, Gilbert was honored by the city of New York. Here he is receiving the Bronze Medal of the city of New York from former mayor Abe Beame.

POPULARITY PLUS. Gilbert, peering through a bunch of his teammates' sticks in the fourth Madison Square Garden, became one of the most popular Rangers of all time. He had a great relationship with the fans, and members of the Rangers Fan Club often voted him "the most popular Ranger on and off the ice." He earned it.

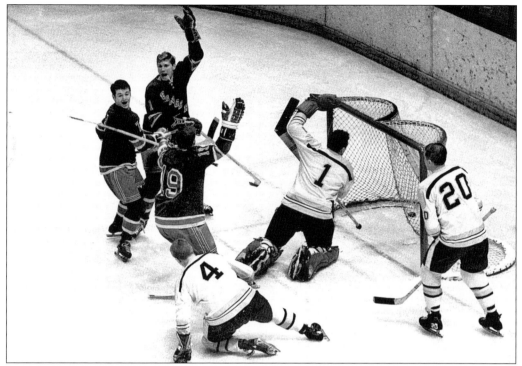

"GOAL-A-GAME." Late in the 1967–1968 season, the Goal-a-Game Line was was formed. "That was one of the best moves I ever made in hockey," mused general manager and coach Emile Francis. This is one of the line's earliest goals, a Jean Ratelle tally against Boston netminder Eddie Johnston at the third Madison Square Garden. Rod Gilbert (in the center) and Vic Hadfield joined the celebration. Boston's Bobby Orr did not.

THIRTY YEARS LATER. The Goal-a-Game Line is reunited on Rod Gilbert Night, March 9, 1977, at the Garden. Jean Ratelle (on the left) and Vic Hadfield (with crutches) greet Gilbert's father, Gabriel, at center ice. It was only the second time in team history (Harry Howell was the first) that an active player was so honored. Gilbert was moved to tears several times during the ceremony.

ROD GILBERT NIGHT

SOUVENIR PROGRAM/MARCH 9, 1977
MADISON SQUARE GARDEN

goal

COVER BOY. The Rangers treated their fans to a special program to honor Rod Gilbert on his big night. Barton Silverman's stunning cover photograph and a 16-page editorial insert celebrated Rod's marvelous career in New York. The programs, 6,000 of them, were gone before the game even began. The team reprinted them and sold mail orders.

GENTLEMAN JEAN. Much in the manner of predecessors Frank Boucher, Neil Colville, and successor Wayne Gretzky, Jean Ratelle was often said to be "as smooth as the ice itself." He was a gracile, highly skilled playmaking center on one of the team's most famous lines ever, the Goal-a-Game Line, with wingers Rod Gilbert and Vic Hadfield. Ratelle was the first Ranger ever to surpass the 100-point barrier in a single season with 109 in 1971–1972.

WINGS LEFT, RANGERS RIGHT. Jean Ratelle, with goal No. 42 of the season, becomes the first Ranger to reach 100 points in a single season on February 20, 1972. He finished with 109 points, still a team record. Ratelle broke his ankle late that season, dealing a crippling blow to the team's chances for a Stanley Cup title. They lost to the Boston Bruins in a six-game final. (Photograph by Paul Bereswill.)

SALUTING RATELLE. The Madison Square Garden message board, precursor of today's multimedia, center-hung scoreboard, salutes Ratelle's record-breaking achievement. Linemates Ratelle, Hadfield, and Gilbert finished third, fourth, and fifth, respectively, on the NHL scoring list that season. (Photograph by Paul Bereswill.)

STANDING TALL. Captain Vic Hadfield seemingly has the Madison Square Garden ice to himself after becoming the first Ranger ever to score 50 goals in a single season on April 2, 1972, the final game of the season. Hadfield scored twice that afternoon against Montreal Canadiens goaltender Denis DeJordy. His mark stood for 22 years until Adam Graves broke it with 52 goals in 1993–1994. (Photograph by Melchior diGiacomo.)

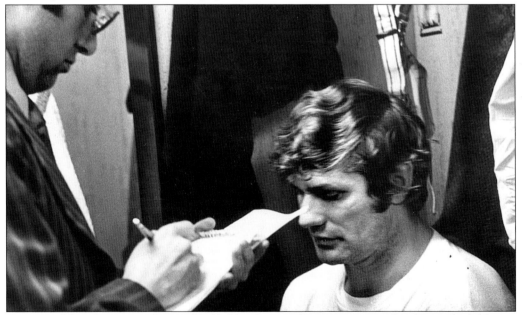

THUMBS UP. A contemplative Hadfield, almost always amongst the best of clubhouse interviews, discusses his 50-goal accomplishment with reporters. Hadfield reached the milestone despite painfully playing the last few weeks of the schedule with two badly injured thumbs. The Rangers made the Stanley Cup finals that season only to lose to the Boston Bruins. (Photograph by Melchior diGiacomo.)

HADFIELD GOES AT IT. In addition to his scoring prowess on the Goal-a-Game Line, left wing Vic Hadfield (being restrained by the officials) was a big fan favorite on account of his willingness to mix it up when necessary. One of Hadfield's frequent targets was Montreal's great center Henri Richard (No. 16).

"BULLDOG" BILLY. Even more than his linemates on the "Bulldog Line," Walter Tkaczuk at center and Dave Balon, and later, Steve Vickers at left wing, right wing Billy Fairbairn looked and played like a bulldog. With a low center of gravity and a tenacious style, he delighted in killing penalties. Not unlike his predecessor of 40 years or so, Murray Murdoch, when Fairbairn was on the ice, goals against were rarely scored.

TOWER OF POWER. Fairbairn's center on the Bulldog Line was Walt Tkaczuk, and physically he was probably the strongest Ranger of his era. Born in Germany but raised in Canada, Tkaczuk was a clever playmaker and nearly impossible to knock off the puck. Tkaczuk ranks fifth on the team's all-time scoring list.

OPPOSITES ATTRACT. Their styles were dead opposite of each other, so they rarely played on the same line. Yet Glen Sather (on the left) and the Rangers' all-time leading scorer, Rod Gilbert, were Ranger teammates for just over three seasons in the early 1970s. A defensive specialist and an ace penalty killer, Sather scored 18 goals and 42 points in 188 games as a Blueshirt.

GLIB GLEN. Long known for his quick and sharp sense of humor, Sather always kept his teammates in a "loosey goosey" frame of mind. "He who dies with the most toys wins" was a favorite bromide he would tell just about anyone who would listen.

"STEMMER" LISTENED. Hardly a slouch himself when it came to clubhouse humor, Peter Stemkowski, the self-proclaimed "Polish Prince," listened to Sather. His usual reply: "He who dies with the most toys is still dead."

OVERTIME HEARTBREAKER. J.P. Parise (No. 12) of the New York Islanders put a dagger into the hearts of Rangers fans everywhere—and knocked the Blueshirts out of the playoffs—when he scored at the 0:11 mark of overtime against Eddie Giacomin on April 11, 1975. At the time, it was the fastest overtime goal in NHL history. It is still the second fastest. (Photograph by Bruce Bennett.)

THE EYES HAVE IT. Emile Francis's eyes could barely focus as he faced the press after what to this day is still called "the Parise Game." Francis said, "I knew, as a team, we were done after that. It was simple. We had run out of chances to win." (Photograph by Bruce Bennett.)

TRADING PLACES. Three of hockey's biggest stars at the time—Phil Esposito, Jean Ratelle, and Brad Park—were teammates and table-mates at the NHL All-Star festivities in 1973 in New York. They did not know it at the time of course, but two and a half years later, they were part of one of the biggest trades in NHL history. Park and Ratelle went to Boston. Esposito headed to Manhattan. In the long term, the Bruins won the trade. (Photograph courtesy of Paul Kanow Collection.)

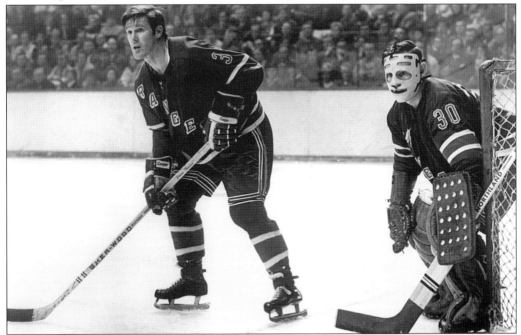

THE STRONGEST RANGER? Sometimes hailed as the strongest player in NHL history, Tim Horton's Ranger career was a short one, only 93 games over two seasons. Yet the heady defenseman contributed greatly. "Tim was a captain without being captain," said Vic Hadfield, the real captain at the time. "He taught us an awful lot." Sadly, Horton's life was also a short one. He died in an automobile accident on Valentine's Day 1974.

HONORING A PIONEER. In 1966, the Rangers established the Lester Patrick Trophy to honor their first general manager and coach Lester Patrick, the man who built the Original Rangers and ran them for 20 years. The award, created by longtime Rangers president Bill Jennings, recognizes "outstanding service to hockey in the United States." Emile Francis (on the left), the team's longtime general manager and coach, was instrumental in the development of the award. Here, he greets the great Gordie Howe, the 1967 recipient of the trophy.

LOCKHART LAUDED. Native New Yorker Tommy Lockhart won the third Lester Patrick Award in 1968. Emile Francis was on hand to help Lockhart celebrate at Toots Shor's legendary restaurant on 52nd Street. Lockhart was the "father of amateur hockey" at Madison Square Garden and was the Rangers' longtime business manager.

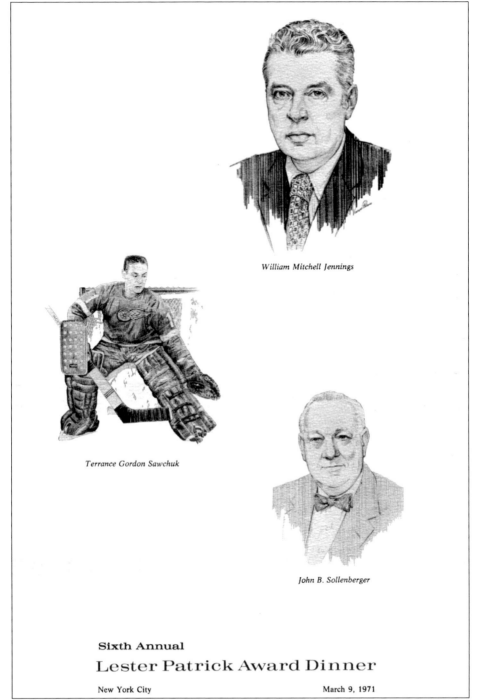

William Mitchell Jennings

Terrance Gordon Sawchuk

John B. Sollenberger

Sixth Annual

Lester Patrick Award Dinner

New York City   March 9, 1971

NEW YORK AFFAIRS. The Lester Patrick Dinner has had numerous formats and venues over the years. But for 15 years, from 1966 to 1980, it was strictly a New York affair, usually in the month of March. Aside from the NHL's annual congress each June, it drew the widest assortment of hockey people each year. The 1971 event honored William Jennings, Terry Sawchuk, and John Sollenberger.

CRAFTY "CAT." Whether he was behind the bench, behind his desk, or behind a draft table microphone, Emile "the Cat" Francis was an artful and resourceful hockey executive. Emile's best draft selections were probably Steve Vickers (1971), Rick Middleton (1973), and Ron Greschner and Dave Maloney (1974).

"OUR LAST CHANCE." By his own admission, Eddie Giacomin was crestfallen when the Rangers lost, four games to three, to the Philadelphia Flyers in the 1974 Stanley Cup semifinals. "It was our last chance, I knew that," Giacomin said. "That one really hurt." Flyers center Terry Crisp consoled Giacomin following game seven at the Spectrum in Philadelphia. The Flyers went on to win the Stanley Cup. (Photograph by Dan Baliotti.)

Eight

A LITTLE BIT OF EVERYTHING

BENCH BEDLAM. The 1982–1983 season was a so-so year for the Rangers. The team finished at .500 with a record of 35-35-10 and lost a playoff division final series to the Islanders. But a late-season goal sent the Rangers bench into euphoria. Celebrating are, from left to right, Don Maloney, Kent-Erik Andersson, Anders Hedberg, Rob McClanahan, Nick Fotiu, Ron Greschner, and Bill Baker. (Photograph by Rich Pilling.)

GIACOMIN LOSES IT. It was eerie; almost surreal. The tears flowed freely for popular goalie Eddie Giacomin on the night of November 2, 1975, just three days after being claimed on waivers by the Detroit Red Wings, ending a 10-year run on Broadway. "One of the toughest days of my life, and certainly the most emotional," Giacomin confided. The fans were raucous in their support for their hero. The Red Wings won 6-4. (Photograph by Bruce Bennett.)

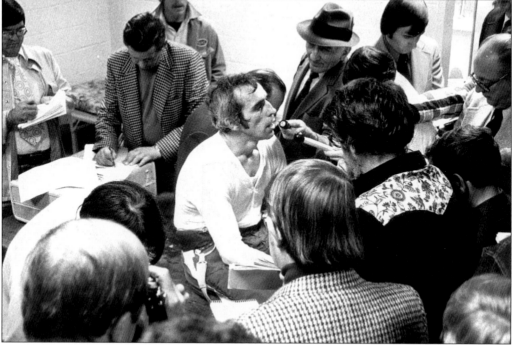

EDDIE EXPLAINS. Clearly drained and spent, a sweat-soaked Giacomin described his feelings to the assembled New York press corps. "You know, I had never been in this room [the visitors' dressing room] before tonight," he quipped. "It sure feels strange." (Photograph by Bruce Bennett.)

A NEW BROOM. New general manager John Ferguson wanted a new look for his 1976–1977 Rangers, so he ordered new uniforms for his club. The author hosted the media conference to introduce the new threads, the home and away versions of which were displayed on mannequins. The uniforms were a bust. The players hated them, and the team quickly reverted to their old duds after two seasons.

THEY CALLED HIM "MURDER." Despite a social calendar that was always full, baby-faced right wing Don Murdoch was one of the most popular Rangers of the "new uniform era." "I played hard and I lived hard, there is no doubt about that. But I had a great time in New York and am proud of my time there." "Murder" is one of only two Rangers to score five goals in one game; Mark Pavelich is the other.

A FAST STARTER. Drafted when he was only 18 years of age, defenseman Dave Maloney spent parts of two seasons with the Providence Reds of the American Hockey League before he got the call to play for New York. On October 11, 1978, the Rangers made him the youngest captain in team history. He was 22 at the time. (Photograph by Melchior diGiacomo.)

FAST STARTER II. Left wing Don Maloney's debut with the Rangers was certainly an auspicious one. He scored a goal on his very first shot on February 14, 1979, against the Boston Bruins. He was the key to the Rangers' brilliant run to the Stanley Cup finals that year, scoring 20 points in the playoffs, then a record for a rookie. He was the MVP of the 1984 All-Star Game in New Jersey and scored a memorable playoff goal in the final minute of regulation time against the Islanders in 1984. (Photograph by Melchior diGiacomo.)

THEY TOOK MANHATTAN. One day after signing with the Rangers, Swedish-born superstars Ulf Nilsson (on the left) and Anders Hedberg and their wives took Manhattan by storm on June 6, 1978. Their itinerary was a packed one and they went to Rockefeller Plaza (across from St. Patrick's Cathedral), behind the counters at Tiffany & Company, on the floor of the New York Stock Exchange, and to the Ninth Avenue food markets. (Photograph by Jerry Liebman.)

BAT BOYS. Judging from their grips, it is apparent that Nilsson (on the left) and Hedberg were certainly better suited for hockey than baseball. Joe Torre, then manager of the New York Mets, was far more comfortable with the lumber. "The Swedes were like a Christmas present, a real bonus," recalled teammate John Davidson. "The publicity alone they got from that tour of New York was amazing."

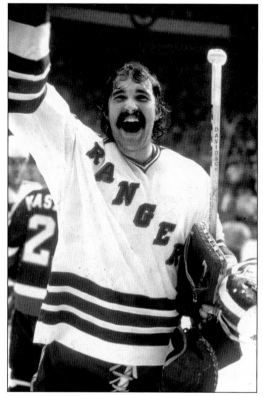

JUBILATION FOR "J.D." Madison Square Garden was rocking at its loudest on May 8, 1979, as the Rangers eliminated the New York Islanders 2-1 in a six-game Stanley Cup semifinal series. It was on to the finals for the first time in seven years. John Davidson, a stalwart in goal, was as throaty as the fans in celebrating the triumph.

EVERYBODY WAS ON BOARD. Seemingly, all of New York City jumped on the 1979 bandwagon. The Rangers were front- and back-page news for a week. The euphoria did not last all that long, as the Montreal Canadiens eliminated the Rangers in the finals, four games to one.

AT CITY HALL. Just a few days after being eliminated by the Canadiens, the Rangers were still basking in the glow of their run to the finals. Mayor Ed Koch invited the team to city hall. General manager and coach Fred Shero (on the left), MSG president "Sonny" Werblin (in the center), and captain Dave Maloney were all presented with keys to the city of New York.

"Doogie" Was Also a Favorite. He was, for six short seasons at least, one of the Rangers' most popular players. Ron Duguay, who played center and right wing, had a distinct, frenetic skating style. It was almost like running on skates rather than gliding. Off the ice, he loved New York and all of its attractions. "I look like a playboy," he once explained. "That's what people think. That doesn't bother me at all."

A Dual Celebration. In 1976, New York City celebrated the bicentennial of the United States. It was also the Rangers' 50th-anniversary season. The team wore a specially created logo that celebrated the bicentennial and the Rangers. The combined logo was used just about everywhere: on the uniforms, the ice, team stationery, tickets, even the Zamboni.

"ESPO" GAVE HIS ALL. His best years were behind him, in Boston of course, but for five and a half seasons, superstar Phil Esposito gave his best for the Rangers, scoring 184 goals. He brought his familiar winning attitude along, and the Rangers zipped to the Stanley Cup finals in 1979. Halfway through the 1980–1981 season, he retired. "I knew it was time," he said. He did it his way.

THE FOURTH AND FIFTH. Defenseman Carol Vadnais was the fourth man in the huge swap between the Rangers and the Bruins. Vadnais played seven seasons and 485 games for the Blueshirts. There was a fifth man in the trade. Little-known defenseman Joe Zanussi went from the Rangers to the Bruins and called himself "the fifth wheel" in one of the biggest trades in hockey history.

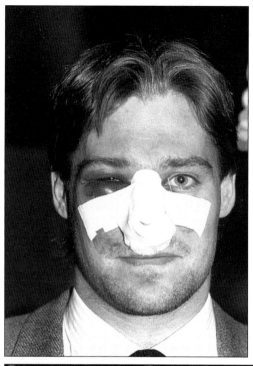

WOUNDED WARRIOR. Injuries are part of every hockey player's career, but few have been as graphic, and undoubtedly painful, as this one endured by left wing Jan Erixon in 1989. An ace defensive forward, Erixon played 10 productive seasons with the Rangers from 1983 to 1993.

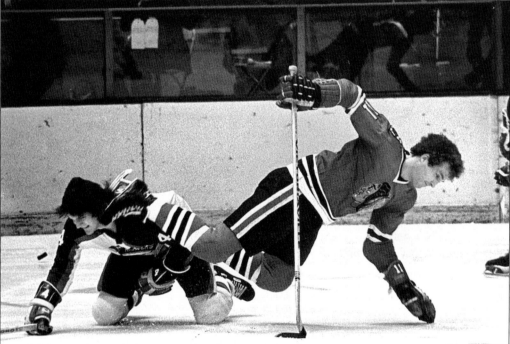

GRESCHNER GETS CLIPPED. With 982 games played, Ron Greschner trails only Harry Howell and Brian Leetch in games played by a Rangers defenseman. Here, Greschner suffers a severe injury to his ear in an unfortunate 1976 collision with the skate of falling Chicago defenseman John Marks.

VICKERS CLAIMS HIS TURF. The area just outside the goal crease was often referred to as Steve Vickers's "office." There were times when the highest-scoring left wing in Rangers history had to claim his turf by force. He does it here with Chicago defenseman Keith Magnuson in 1978.

"NIFTY" WAS SENT PACKING. Was it the worst trade in Rangers history? Well, the man who made it, John Ferguson, certainly thinks so. Ferguson often wailed years later, "Why, oh why did I ever trade Rickey Middleton?" The man he was traded for, Ken Hodge of Boston, scored 23 goals in 96 games with the Rangers. Middleton, known as "Nifty," scored 402 in 881 games with the Bruins. Ouch. Here Middleton, still a Ranger, celebrates a four-goal game against the California Seals on November 17, 1974.

"POTVIN S _ _ _ S". He is, hands down, the most unpopular opposing player ever to play at Madison Square Garden. Peerless defenseman Denis Potvin of the New York Islanders, shown here dueling with Don Maloney, earned the fans' wrath and an unseemly chant that went with it when he cleanly slammed center Ulf Nilsson into the boards at the Garden on February 25, 1979. Nilsson suffered a broken right ankle and really was never quite the same thereafter.

THE "FLOWER" TAKES NEW YORK. His legendary years with the Montreal Canadiens were well behind him, but Rangers fans got a bonus dose of Guy Lafleur's greatness during the 1988–1989 season. General manager Phil Esposito coaxed Lafleur out of retirement and the dashing right wing once again dazzled Garden crowds with his electrifying rushes.

OILERS TO RANGERS. Winners of the Stanley Cup as members of the Edmonton Oilers in 1990 are, from left to right, Kevin Lowe, captain Mark Messier, and Jari Kurri. Six years later, the three were reunited as members of the Rangers in 1995–1996. One thing did not change in six years: Messier was still the captain.

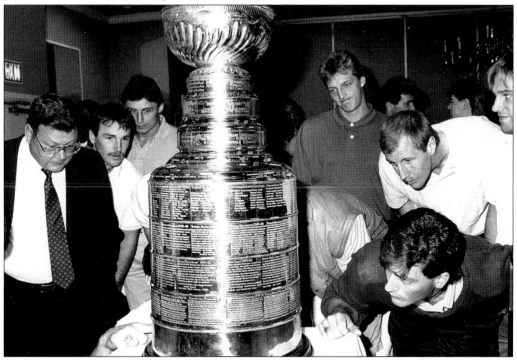

THE ULTIMATE GOAL. In 1986, in his first season as general manager of the Rangers, Phil Esposito brought the Stanley Cup itself to the team's training camp. The younger players, most of whom had never even seen the trophy much less touched it, were in awe. It did not matter. The Rangers finished fourth and were bounced from the Stanley Cup playoffs by the Philadelphia Flyers.

CHANGES, CHANGES. When Esposito took control of the Rangers, change was in the air, every hour, every day. He made a dizzying series of trades and constantly preached his new motto: "No More Waiting." He upgraded the team's travel schedule, and to the surprise of no one, was a "players' guy." He even changed the decades-old method of taking the team picture by

replacing a formally posed shot with a carefree bunch of relaxed players, some in uniform, some in civvies, and some memorabilia. "Espo" himself was front and center. The new picture was fun, but it never sold.

CAPTAIN BARRY. Widely—and somewhat unfairly—heralded as a savior upon his arrival from the Colorado Rockies on November 2, 1979, hulking defenseman Barry Beck was named the Rangers' 19th captain on February 4, 1981. He took over from Walt Tkaczuk, who seemed almost relieved to shed the captaincy and all of its responsibilities. Injuries cut into Barry's playing time, but he spent seven seasons on Broadway.

Nine

THE 1994 SEASON
AND BEYOND

"SLATS" TAKES OVER. He was already in the Hockey Hall of Fame when he got the call to come to New York. Glen Sather arrived on June 1, 2000, and slowly but surely put his personal touch on the Rangers of the new millennium. Sather brought in big names like Eric Lindros, Pavel Bure, Alexei Kovalev, and Bobby Holik as he tried to rebuild the Blueshirts with an eye on past glory. "Slats" left no stone unturned, even putting himself behind the bench to replace the departing Bryan Trottier.

THE ONE AND ONLY. There has been only one United States–born captain in Rangers history, and that is peerless defenseman Brian Leetch. The remaining 21 Rangers captains were Canadian. Born in Texas and raised in Connecticut, Leetch is arguably the best player the Rangers have ever had. His sparkly resume includes three major NHL trophies, the Calder, the Norris, and the Smythe, and an outspoken love for the city of New York.

"GIVING" IS HIS GAME. Adam Graves is a remarkable left winger, model citizen, and poster-boy really for everything a professional athlete should stand for. Much has been written and broadcast about Graves's cornucopia of charity activities. Suffice it to say, on the ice or off, he is one of the most giving athletes ever, in any sport.

A CUP-WINNING GOALIE. He is the most recent on a long list of heroes that the Rangers have called goalies over 78 seasons, and one of only two United States–born netminders to spend a considerable period of time with the team (John Vanbiesbrouck was the other). There is one enduring image of Mike Richter that stands out. It is the sweat-soaked Richter's look of pure ecstasy just after the Rangers won the Stanley Cup on June 14, 1994. Richter's look of delight was really for everyone—players and fans alike.

HOCKEY'S GREATEST LEADER. Mark Messier is the greatest leader hockey has ever known. Of course, Messier's glory years were in Edmonton, but he has firmly secured his place in Rangers history, most notably with his astounding guarantee of a victory in game six of the 1994 Conference finals against the Devils. Not only did the captain promise the win, but he sealed it himself, scoring a hat trick in the third period of an amazing 4-2 Rangers win in New Jersey. It was that guarantee and that series that catapulted the Rangers toward their first Stanley Cup in 54 seasons.

BRIAN'S TOPS. Few would argue that dynamic defenseman Brian Leetch is the greatest Ranger ever. For sure, no one can match his list of honors: two Norris Trophies (for best defenseman), one Calder Trophy (rookie of the year), one Smythe Trophy (playoff MVP), one World Cup MVP (shown here), and one Stanley Cup. It does not get any better than that.

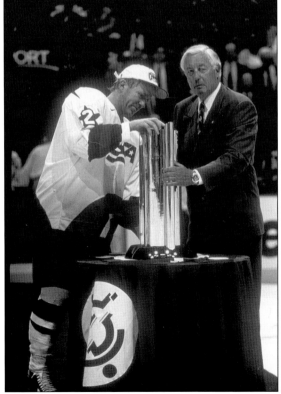

THIS ONE IS FOR YOU. The eyes might have been bloodshot, so they stayed hidden, but there was no mistaking Mark Messier's toothy grin that said "Hallelujah" for Rangers fans around the world. "There is no greater feeling," Messier confided to reporters, "than riding up Broadway and seeing the tickertape come down. I will never forget that." And Rangers fans will never forget what Messier meant to them in 1994: a Stanley Cup.

SMILES FOR NOW. General manager Neil Smith and his new head coach Mike Keenan were all smiles when Keenan took the coaching reins on April 17, 1993. The two were rarely on the same page thereafter, which was probably a discredit to them both. They sometimes bickered anonymously in the press. Despite their differences, they won the Stanley Cup. In a messy divorce, Keenan eventually resigned after the one championship season.

LINDROS ARRIVES, FINALLY.
While the trade for Eric Lindros, shown here winning the Hart Trophy as the NHL's MVP in 1995, surely raised some eyebrows—and doubtless some hackles as well—the move was "pure Glen Sather." The old hockey axiom was at work here: the team that gets the best player wins. The Rangers got the best player, even if it was nine years after they wanted him, but lost out to the Philadelphia Flyers in 1992.

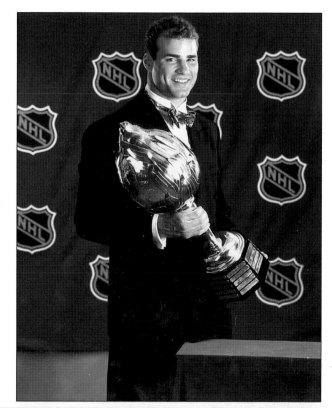

THREE BIG GUYS. Among the first to welcome the "Big Guy" Eric Lindros to New York in August 2001 were two other big guys, broadcasters John Davidson (on the left) and Sam Rosen. Lindros had a quick impact on his new team, scoring 73 points in 72 games for the 2001–2002 season. (Photograph courtesy of George Kalinsky).

STILL GREAT. He is simply the greatest hockey player who ever lived, and the Rangers got three spine-tingling seasons out of "the Great One," Wayne Gretzky, from 1996 to 1999. Gretzky certainly had not lost much of his magic, scoring 249 points in 234 games. He even got to play a season (1996–1997) with his old pal Mark Messier.

GOING OUT GREAT. Fittingly enough, No. 99 Wayne Gretzky chose 1999 for his retirement. Mark Messier, Brian Leetch, and Jeff Beukeboom joined "the Great One" for the ceremony at Madison Square Garden. Gretzky said, "It was a privilege to finish my career in New York, maybe the greatest city the world has ever known."

FOR SURE, THEY CALLED. Scotty Bowman is the most successful coach in NHL history with 1,244 victories. There is little doubt that the Rangers have inquired about his services, and probably on more than one occasion. Nine Stanley Cups speak for themselves.

PROLIFIC LENSMAN. In all likelihood, Bruce Bennett has photographed more hockey games and hockey-related events than anyone else in history. From Stanley Cups, to All-Star Games, to any other game, Bennett has done it all. His work has appeared in hockey publications of all kinds, both nationally and internationally.

DiGiacomo and a Friend. Internationally known photojournalist Melchior diGiacomo, shown here with Chris Evert, has a vast array of hockey photographs, many of which are featured in this work. DiGiacomo's keen eye and style produced thousands of excellent hockey images.

The Garden's Ace. For parts of five decades since 1965, George Kalinsky has been a fixture at Madison Square Garden number three and MSG number four. With great style and flair, he has photographed more MSG events and happenings than any other person in history, and he has done it with prize-winning skill and grace.

THE DYNAMIC DUO. For nearly two decades, Sam Rosen (on the left) and John Davidson (on the right) have been lighting up the airwaves on Rangers telecasts. Rosen's up-to-the-second play-by-play and Davidson's always-on-the-money observations have been a treat for the Blueshirt faithful to behold. (Photograph courtesy of Madison Square Garden Network.)

Off ice, pillars of virtue

Rangers there when city needed them

IT'S going to be different here in New York this week; we are going to view life again through a different prism. We will be reminded of where we were a year ago, reminded of how we responded to the sneak attack on our city, our country and our values. Maybe it will be healthy for us. Maybe it will prove cathartic. Maybe it will reinvigorate us to face the challenges that most certainly lie ahead.

It is going to be different in this space today, too. No yelling. No screaming. No finger-pointing. No lectures. No sources. A timeout from all of that. There is always going to be time for all of that.

During a season, however, there isn't always time to recognize the best in the people who play hockey. We don't so much as cover the people as we do the athletes, we don't evaluate the individuals as much as the performances, we grade organizations on little other than winning percentage.

But not today.

It is important today to recognize the Rangers for the way they embrace their responsibility as citizens of our city. The organization has always been community-minded, the Garden has always encouraged its professional athletes to give something back — Dave Checketts may never have won a title overseeing the Garden, but his Cheering for Children program is a legacy more truly meaningful than any trophy or two — and the players have always responded.

The Rangers of the last five years haven't always been good players, but overwhelmingly they have been good people and excellent ambassadors for New York. Last year, when that was not always an easy burden, they were at their best; their most altruistic. The Rangers don't only play here, they live here, more than half in the city, that alone making the team unique among the eight that play under the New York banner.

Mark Messier provided brilliant leadership as captain, knowing instinctively how to connect to those needing support and comfort. Ron Low, torn the way the rest of us were about going about our daily business in the face of national and civic tragedy, handled a complex situation with grace and strength. The Rangers stopped winning halfway through the year but they never stopped contributing to the city's recovery efforts. They never do.

A year ago the Garden and Rangers set aside a section in the stands for our Hometown Heroes to recognize the invaluable citizens who protect us every day of the year. Their recognition over the PA system and on the scoreboard invariably prompted emotional standing ovations that really were the highlight of the home season. I hope the program remains intact this season.

The Islanders responded magnificently, the Devils did their part, all around the league, the NHL, its players, its teams; they represented themselves and their sport like champions. The Rangers, more affected as a team than any other, with homes and apartments just blocks away from firehouses that lost lives, led the effort.

Today, it seems to me, it is appropriate to remind everyone.

■

Chris Ferraro is one of our own, born and raised in Port Jefferson with his twin brother, **Peter;** played a bit with the Rangers, played a bit with the Islanders.

When the Caps open training camp at Piney Orchard on Friday, Chris Ferraro will be on the ice for the first time since last Oct. 16, the day his own world was hit; the day that his wife of three months, Jennifer, was diagnosed with stomach cancer.

Chris Ferraro was in L.A. and had played against the Kings after having just been recalled from Portland of the AHL. When he returned to his hotel room after the match, he received the news. He left the team immediately, ending his season so he could be by his wife's side through the arduous recovery process.

Jennifer Ferraro is 31. They took her stomach out six months ago. They found cancer in her intestines. As her treatment continues, she perseveres bravely. She lives life. So does Chris Ferraro, who returns to the rink on Friday.

MAKING A DIFFERENCE: Mark Messier and the Rangers may have been disappointments on the ice the last few years, but their charitable work and community efforts went above and beyond the call of duty, Larry Brooks says.

Reuters photos

STEPPING UP. After the terrorist attacks in New York on September 11, the Rangers stepped up their already strong activities on behalf of charities helping the cause. One of the most striking images of this period is this photograph of captain Mark Messier standing at center ice at the Garden with the hat of fireman Ray Downey.